WITHDRAWN

INSTRUCTIONS FOR VIEWING A SOLAR ECLIPSE

The Wesleyan Poetry Program: Volume 61

Instructions for Viewing

a Solar Eclipse

By DAVE KELLY

WESLEYAN UNIVERSITY PRESS

Middletown, Connecticut

SALEM COLLEGE LIBRARY
WINSTON-SALEM, N. C.

PS
3561
E 393
I 5

Copyright © 1966, 1967, 1968, 1969, 1970, 1971, 1972 by
David M. Kelly

Acknowledgement is gratefully made to the following
periodicals, in the pages of which some of the poems in this
volume were first published: *Ann Arbor Review, Choice,
The Experimentalist, Hearse, Lillabulero, The Nation,
Nickel Review, Northeast, Poetry Review, Prairie Schooner,
Pyramid, Runcible Spoon, Sepharim, Sumac,* and *Westigan
Review.*
    The poems "Dogs," "Easy Rider Where Did You Sleep
Last Night?," "Mira, Mira," "Some Three-Line Stanzas,"
"The Walls," and "Winter Walking Fields" were first pub-
lished in *Lillabulero.*

Hardbound: ISBN 0-8195-2061-6

Paperback: ISBN 0-8195-1061-0

Library of Congress catalog card number: 78-184365

Manufactured in the United States of America

First edition

To George Chambers

94666

CONTENTS

I TURNER'S THESIS

TURNER'S THESIS: SONNET FOR THE DONNER PARTY
or
THEY WENT THATAWAY

So they all went west with hope in their hearts
and their children strapped to the saddles
with bits of furniture locked in their teeth
they stopped further away every night
and the sun closer and they grew beards
and said things like "this is the place."

Until the wolves had stood around their fires
one night too many and they were hungry
in mountains where they cooked the children
dead from exposure in their hopeless pots.
When they finally got there the water
in their new ocean was far from blue.

They laughed, ate baby sandwiches, grabbed
rusted hammers and built Disneyland and Watts.

11

SALEM COLLEGE LIBRARY
WINSTON-SALEM, N. C.

THE GENERATION OF LOVE

This is the generation of love:
these are the lovers with sand in their teeth,
their words caught between dry lips,
the doves in olive trees, their wings torn
by branches; the generation of love is at play.

These are the words of the generation of love:
the machine gunning of soft eyes,
the smiles pressed between pages of books,
the hard coin of promises, the end
of laughter interned for the duration.

These are the faces of the generation of love:
shadows flying up gray walls to hide
in the leaves of trees, hands growing fur
and eyes, teeth finding homes in throats
and old men in offices signing blank paper.

The generation of love goes where it is sent,
debarks from dark planes in the rain at night,
drops from the clouds with heat in its hands,
watches children grab their bellies and fall
face down eyes blank in puddles of red mud.

The generation of love is The Virgin in a trench.
The generation of love is an angel kissing wounds.
Torn open by the elders at play, the generation
of love sits in a bare room waiting for orders
and invents strange new ways to make rain fall.

This is the song of the generation of love:
the coughing of old men alone in their rooms,
the laughter of children forgetting their
fathers' names, metal spoons stirring
sour liquors in steel cans in the night.

The world explodes, the doves drop from trees
like stained snow falling from a bleeding cloud.
Shadows lift themselves on broken wings
and fall back to the ground in limp piles.
The generation of love sleeps on concrete

hills, under steel stars children crawl
broken into heaps of dead leaves and the hand
of a clown touches fire to them as they
sleep. This is the generation of love this
is the tournament of the shattered smile.

This is the last dream of an age of lovers.
This is the speech of a ripped tongue
stabbing the throat of the soft voices.
These are our torn eyes on the wet ground
in the broken house of the generation of love.

AFTER READING THE LAST 3 POEMS OF MIKLOS RADNOTI

It's been 23 years since that all happened
and pines grow through the ribcages of dead Jews
in the Hungarian woods and yesterday a letter

from a friend
scolded

"NO MORE POLITICS!"

to be in my poems.
Of course we are
children of peace

and there are no more bullets
snapping the cords of young lives

to write our poems about.

Silence has danced over the world since 1944
like a blanket of pale lunar moths.

It's a kind of smile
you see a lot these days,

on the guy at the office
who was at the same pill party

you were last Friday, on
the phys ed teacher

when he puts an arm around
the shoulder of the halfback

who belongs to the same
shooting club

and patriotic organization
and on the face

of the black professor
when the campus black

revolutionary walks up
to the cafeteria table

and in the eyes
of the pink professor

when the campus white
revolutionary

walks up to the
cafeteria table and on

the creased foreheads of the dean
and the vice-president for anything

and the police chief after a good weekend
when any of them

looks at the others and
seen it before? Why sure, it's

the same grin you used to
slip your favorite highschool

buddy when he gave you that note
in class that said,

"If you got any last night,
Smile."

It is morning and the trees have gone home
The mouse crawls out of the wall to the cat
I sit in a portrait looking at my children
The clouds fall from themselves to the ground

Everywhere I look red is screaming from skies
The old men who taught me are all dead
The young are sent out with their coffins
And the coffins never come home alone

Wherever I go the ground is wet and cold
No one who lies in it ever gets up
The trees fly by their eyes wide with fear
A torn scalp crawls slowly over a face

A crow holds the leg of an owl in its claw
Ice seals the dead eyelid of a horse
A child eating candy loads his rifle and waits
while voices of cracked drums fill the air

Naked legs of angels become burned roots
They wrap around each other like basketed snakes
Wreaths of flowers fall from doors and scream
The sun is an eye with a nail struck through it

A fist drives into a face that laughs and vanishes
When it draws back the knuckles are raw
Tall heavy men shudder in corners of rooms
where the bones of hands play an endless piano

The world dressed in brown stumbles over a hill
Smoke in its teeth in its eyes in its hands
On Monday I look for shelter for my careful life
On Tuesday death walks to the polls and votes

Yesterday we killed the last man who believed.
Now we can begin looking at the stones in the
bottoms of our bowls and the children dying

under our fingernails and the smoke growing
out of our eyes and filling the empty air.

Today we can begin wandering where there is no
place to walk. We can swim through concrete.

Tomorrow we can watch it all take place and
wonder why we were not in time for anything.

We can wonder what there was that we once called
us and where it has gone in the April rain.

Forever now our eyes will fail to meet.

We have forgotten the songs that might have saved us.
We have used up the words that could open a door
and we must learn to move now without a direction.

There is only a desert and a tree without leaves

and even the desert is no longer ours
and even the tree has turned its back on us.

The last dance of the elephants
in the straw circle, the roaring lights,
the fat, sweating forehead of the tuba
player, see how the children are laughing.
Can there be dignity still come from Africa?

The brown hand of the candy man twists
the white cardboard cone into the ex-
ploding pink webs in the machine. We
watch through the glass. His arm is
bare to the elbow. Snakes dance on it.

The unborn swim in jars. The freaks smile.
The money rolls in. Surprising how young
the nudes are. Corn Cobb smuggles a
camera into the burlesque tent, gets some
good shots of pussy for his locker door.

It's a bright light brass band evening.
Kids stumble off the rides and get sick.
The eyes behind the counters are hard.
Mine snarl back, pretend to know the same
towns, to know what hey rube means.

I break five balloons at the dart game.
You are proud, your arm through mine.
I pretend it was easy, tuck the stuffed
doll under my left arm. We walk off.
Should I climb in with the lions?

The ballerina on the high wire is afraid.
Her brother died this way last year
and in the same town. The people flock
to the show hoping it will happen again.
On the wire their fear smells like money.

In the morning there will be nothing here
but dust and horse turds. The people
from town will be sleeping, ticket stubs
in trousers over chairs, the dangers they
bought locked in boxes rolling out of town.

EASY RIDER WHERE DID YOU SLEEP LAST NIGHT?
YOUR SHOES AIN'T BUTTONED, CLOTHES DON'T FIT YOU RIGHT

She walked into their room with the same smile
on her soft face she'd walked out of mine with
and undressed and lay down on their beds too
and loved them one at a time and walked down
the hall to somebody else's room. It was her
idea to call it loving, we had a lot of other
words for it but we shot deer and she didn't.

In the whore house in Nogales, Mexico, the girl's
name was Lupe. She said she was from Mazatlan,
from the mountains, from a small fishing village.
She said she was from everywhere but home.
She hummed to herself as she took off her clothes
and crossed herself as she got in bed. Her boy-
friend pared his nails in the bar across the street.

The girl in the House of Correction looked down.
Looked down at the priest on the curb and smiled.
"Is there anything I can get you?" he called.
Her long black hair filled the steel window
and her eyes disappeared into the room.
"Bring me a good fuck," he heard back.

The girl with the pale, narrow face drove her car
into a space behind the five-story house.
The men drifted out to the lot like hungry ants.
It rained when she drove into the parking lot.
It rained when she shook out her hair and drove home.
Her father sat in his chair reading his evening paper.

The girl in the room at the end of the hall is smiling.
The boys in the line outside tell dirty jokes and laugh.
It is raining in her eyes somewhere behind the smile
in the dark room that is part of the empty street.
In the street a guitar is playing and a cracked voice
sings, "I have slept in the pines where the sun never
shines and the cold and the cold winds blow."

THE NIGHT OF THE TERRIBLE LADDERS

The night of the terrible ladders;
insomniac taxis crawl
inch by inch on wet tar,
the eyes of widows
follow the blinking signs
on the road from dusk until morning
and the children smother in their hot beds.

I light a cigarette beneath a street lamp.
An old woman watches me from the steel
of the fire escape she sits on.
The radio plays in the room behind her.
I look up into her dented eyes
and we follow each other
into the night of the terrible ladders.

The street limps down itself to the corner.
Under the lights the women are turning,
waiting to follow the strangers home.
A pigeon lies next to the curb
singing what no one can understand.
The terrible ladders lead into themselves;
it is night and I follow them.

I walk past the one-eyed man
smiling at me from cracked glass,
past the staggered hands of cripples
reaching for my laughter on hot streets,
past the broken smiles of angels
turning for money beneath smoked lights.
I follow the ladders home.

It is the night of terrible ladders.
It is the night of rabid things;
of rats seeking the flesh of children,
of shadows eating the stench from steel cans,
of dark wings circling above lights,
of women fleeing lovers in darkness,
of blind men leading me home.

The terrible ladders cover the rocks,
the sea cannot wash them away;
the sea with its layer of garbage
lies at the end of this street,
catches the city and washes it back
over the street of the broken bird,
over my face as it looks for home.

The night of the terrible ladders;
the drunken lights of taxis
wash over the gutter of birds,
pass over the face of the widow
sweating on her steel perch
and touch the skirts of the sea
and the women turning on corners.

The terrible ladders follow me nowhere.
The terrible ladders follow me home.

Am I Irish?
I am not Irish.
They wait for me in the alley
but I will make it.

Their teeth whistle at me
as I run by.

They catch up with me
and I stand on the corner
holding a bashful smile
with a pickle on it

in the palm of my sweating hand.

Am I a Spanish corsair?
I am not Spanish.
Garlics ripen at the ends
of strings hanging in the kitchen.

I stumble through the room
brushing the pepper gourds aside.

You wait, naked, on your back
in a barrel of onions.
I fall laughing into you
and we fuck food

till the stinking room disappears.

I am late for school.
The teacher disapproves.

Her eyes are the way
old gum feels under strange chairs.
The teacher doesn't love me.
The girl in the next seat

doesn't love me. Desperate,
I stare into my book.
Give me a name,

for Christ sake give me a name.

DREAM COWBOY

On the track behind the high-school building
the slight body of a boy sprawls against the ground
his arms folded across his eyes. A drop of light
falls from the moon and on his wine-colored
jacket. The hard columns of blue legs straddle
him and punch up into the torso of a fat cop
leaning back against the sky, chewing a breath
mint and blowing the smoke off his .38 special.

II THE EXPERTS

It is noon.
A whistle blows from the top of the gray tower.
The sergeant sits on a railroad tie
eating his lunch

(liverwurst, black bread
and a pickle)

facing the mound
made by the woman
lying dead,

her back broken,
one eye staring into
a fly cleaning

itself in the dirt
before her.

I am the only one behind him.

I am holding a shovel
staring at the short hair
on the back of his head.

I lift
the shovel.

A shot.

I have forgotten the guard
behind me.

Two weeks later
I am stillborn
with both arms missing

on the South Side
in Chicago.

A pimp
in a silk shirt
pares his nails.

Finally
I make it,
whole,
white,

and something of a Christian.

I write poems
in the kitchen

while the baby
plays in the dog's dish

on the floor.

THE CASTLE OF THE DROWNING HERMIT

The eyes of the blonde girl drown
in the bottom of the glass, her voice
melts in the smoke in the dark
room, the hands of pearls wave
around her as she chokes in the weeds.

God, the priest cries, God I have
been taking out your garbage too
long, I want the petals of flesh to
open for me, I want to die digging
my hands into soft pink thighs.

The drums thud the children march
into the dirt field they are tied
to posts they are raped by baboons
they are shot by their fathers and
photographed with their eyes closed.

The surgeons wear their white coats.
They cluster around a table, sleeves
splashed with red as severed
legs and arms fly out around them.
Singing they revive a corpse of God.

The sea boils, fish drown in it
sucking for air. Bathers are scorched
black on the beaches while the
sand fuses into molten glass. How
many years since the last world?

How many years till the next one ends?
This is a problem for mathematic
genius, how many screaming souls can
be twisted into a small jar, if you
boil them down they will all fit.

A small boy sits in a corner feeding
mice to his cat. Cigarettes are lit.
Coffee is poured. The parents lean back
to watch. The first bone broken is
small and makes very little noise.

The sirens are ringing over Hanoi.
Americans have been sighted flying
north from a spot some distance away.
In fifteen minutes they will be over
the city and their bellies will open
like bloodless sores, a mistake has

been made, they are not bombing oil
or the rails where there are no humans,
only soldiers and military trains,
they are bombing the schools and cities.
The eyes of the children fail to believe.

On a piece of dry dirt in Oklahoma
Norma Thirtyacres sits on rough boards
in the reservation school and listens
while the thin white lady tells about
heritage as Norma rolls the louse she's

caught in a ball with the ball of
her thumb. We have been told we are
right. We forget the holes in the speakers'
throats and keep the words they speak.
In the projects in South Side Chicago, B. J.
and Willie come up behind Bobbie Jo Jones

and break his skull against the fountain
as he drinks. A young psychopath lies
in a hospital bed on the other side of town
while eight nurses scream in his eyes.
There have been thirty-five gangland
executions in Boston the last thirty months

and the jelly falls on children in Hanoi,
burning them like so much screaming paper.
In Chicago the surviving nurses change
bedpans and take pulses and on the South
Side a local drinking fountain gives off
the taste of brain for at least a week.

Being civilized, you first think
that the long wooden tube in his mouth
is a blowgun, for shooting poisoned
darts at Alan Ladd, but when you
read on you learn that it's a
flute, a wooden flute as long as
his wife he holds in his mouth and
spends about half his waking
hours playing. This isn't many, as
he gets, it says, at least twelve
hours sleep a night and naps frequent-
ly besides. His song on the flute is
always the same: three notes and a
pause or slap of the foot on the dirt
floor of the concert hall, then three
notes and another pause or slap.
This is the only time he ever slaps
anything. He doesn't have wars, and
his worst sin is to accuse another
of a sin like arson, theft, adultery
or missing one of the three notes.
When he isn't playing the flute
he sings, usually a song that goes,
"whooooooO." He lives to be forty-
five, the magazine tells you, per-
haps dying young because of a lack
of hostility and competition to
harden his edges against. But he
doesn't complain because he doesn't
even know that some people somewhere
else might live to be forty-six.
The article tells you there are no

more than a hundred ten Kalapalo
in the world, but all happy on a game
preserve on the Amazon in the middle
of Brazil, protected against you by
several rivers and a game warden.

THE POOL

There was a place
a pool we all
came down for water

with the moon
above and
shining from it.

Quiet we came
silver and black
different ones of us

from among the trees
the hair of the
women long and

snagged with briars, leaves.
Some dark as the pool
some light as the moon

we, all, naked
walking carefully our
toes pointed straight

and the silence
around us was
from us.

There was a place
a pool we all
came down for water.

THE EXPERTS

The wild grape vines are choking the young trees
and will never themselves bear fruit.
The banty man in the hard yellow helmet
squints up at the pine and tells us
it will last for years but the basswood
will crash into our roof when it dies.

He is a tree expert and we believe him.
Other experts surround us in their trucks.
One digs a well, another builds a pump
and another tastes our water, spits
and tells us we should move our septic tank.

We call another expert to do that job.
I am a home owner in short brown pants,
a householder who offers beer to the painters.
I spend the mornings writing letters to the editor
while machines crash in the branches of trees
out in the yard with the bruise-shirted experts.

But when I carry out my boards and hammer
they are already breaking for lunch
and they grin at me through their sandwiches
and split apples in halves with their hands.
I stop, pretending to remember something.
Inside I pull the blinds and sleep all day.

They always led their captive
to the same place, a flat runway
at the top of one of their hills
and stripped him there. It was a
death reserved for only the great
warriors among their enemies.
With the wind screaming around
them they stood the man on his
feet and two of them held him
there. Then one would take the
sharpest knife and move behind the
three of them. The holders pulled
his arms out straight and the
man with the knife would slit a
long wedge down the back on each
side by the shoulder bone, always
careful not to cut the heart.
When the back was sliced open
on both sides the man with the
knife would drop the knife and
plunge a hand into each hole
while the other two looked deep
into their prisoner's face for
a certain look of readiness in
the eyes. At a nod from one the
knifer would pull both hands deft-
ly from the slits. Each hand held
a lung and yanked it absolutely
free. The two men dropped their
victim's arms and he would always
run straight down the track, his
elbows pushing behind him to fill

the gaps in his back. They called
them wings. They called the sound
that whistled out his wounds and
mouth the eagle's song. When he
fell they rolled his body down
the hill. The lungs they cooked
and fed to their dogs at night.

I

He walks with
his teeth set
in his mouth

as if
it mattered

as if tomorrow
meant more

than today
as if

he weren't going to die.

He asks where
his office is

as if

he would be there
when he got there

as if the door
wouldn't open

and close for
anyone the same

way. He

lies in his bed
as if he rested

as if

the morning would
bring him childhood

as if the warmth of a blanket
were life.

He smiles at
his friends

as if he knew them.

II

Monday. Tuesday. Wednesday. Thursday. Friday.
The weekend.

Lovers.

Parks.

Children walking.

It rains for hours.
The wind moves up fast

cold and wet from the hills. Lightning
makes the trees smell of smoke.
We all wear gray.

As long as we are quiet we are waterproof.

Sunday is a time
for roasted leg of lamb

Saturday
a memory

in the gray rain.

Don't ask if I know what I mean
don't ask if I can be made to care

for green hills

I sit in a chair

inside

by the drawn shade.

III

We all hurry
to the scenes
of accidents.

The mothers among us
hold up children

to watch, only the professionals
are bored, the police

with their rubber gloves,
ambulance drivers,

and reporters
holding pencils

and small pads.
They exchange greetings,
some of them

haven't seen each
other since the
last death.

Some will buy
each other drinks
in the late day.

Some are looking
for each other's jobs.

I have shared afternoons
with most of them,

I have pitched dirty pennies
at their office walls.

I have also been

torn open
by metal edges.

IV

What are the defenses
you have set against

pain?

What are the sounds you
fill empty nights with?

Do you wonder where your
mind goes when you

sleep or
do you let yourself down
into it like

a coffin given up to
finality, a

resignation of stale flowers?

Each day lies
in front of itself

and is filled with
what each of us comes to

each night frightens us
with what we are

and the attacking voices
of real persons.

Do not be
afraid of

these abstractions, you

are not living
your life, you

are only
reading

a poem.

AND THEN WHAT?

"I think I'll hitchhike around the country for awhile.
Try to find myself."   (overheard)

                    I finally ran into me one night
                    in a pizza joint in Albuquerque.

                    I was drinking Coors and
                    eating the red peppers. "Well kid,

                    here we finally are eh?
                    Hey Nellie, give the kid here

                    a drink. What'll ya have kid?"
                    he said.

                    "Coors," I said, that being
                    what I seemed to be

                    drinking.

THE WALLS

The walls fell down without
giving notice to us or the roof

or the people inside them. The children

cried in the
sudden cold

and snow colored the hair of the mother
and the father with his
large, heavy pipe.

He thought a moment.
That was all there was.

Stars.
Some wind, totally unexpected.

And the children with their cold, endless crying.

The woman's teeth begin chattering.
The man tells her to stop, she is
not good for morale.

It is now that we know there
will be a new way of deciding things.

Cold and warmer were a matter
of thick or thin blood and for laughter.

Now they depend on how fast you can move.

I can move faster than you. We have
a new game to play and with new rules. Hey, look,

the walls are come down.
Isn't it nice?
We are free.

Yes but that would have been nice in summer. Now, how-

ever, we have new games to play. Some
are called dying. Simply

and few people are missed.

FISHING

The first light from the sun
rising at my back touches
the houses on the far shore
of the lake, bringing them
out from the dark trees.

A chill breathes in the air
as I yawn and stoop to turn
the skiff over and pull it
toward the water. My feet
feel the first cold waves.

In the water now, I climb
into the boat and pole off with
an oar from the shallows,
watching the color deepen
and the lake's floor disappear.

I fit an oar into each lock
and my feet against the ridge
on the boat's floor and set
my back against the steady pull.
I angle south down the shore.

The house behind you shadows
you and the dock as I pull
up to it. You hand me your pole
and slide easily from the dock,
feet first into the boat.

I turn the boat out toward
the center of the lake and we
slide back over the weeds and
the rocks till we can't see
the bottom and I rest the oars.

I am not sitting in a skiff
in the middle of a lake. I never
fish but I do row sometimes. I
am sitting at an oak desk in a
house, writing a false poem.

DOGS

for William Matthews

I like to watch
the dogs in the yard.

The three of them,
large and made to

look like wolves
catch each other's
fur in their teeth

and throw each other
through the long beach grass.

There is an understanding

it seems
that only the youngest
gets hurt.

At night there are
fine silences

between them.

III IF THERE IS MORE

IF THERE IS MORE

There is a word
I would have you
hear instead of

killing me but that
means this also
that I am for you

to do as you must
knowing what would
be enough

it is this simply
that for you I
turn my back

to you I lay my
arms at my
sides and my

hands are bare
if there is more I
do not have it

POISON WHEAT

The squirrel in the roof is screaming.
His feet pull at the beams in the wall.
Acorns fall around him to the floor
and his throat works around dry pain.

Yesterday I put the poison in the attic.
Open boxes of fire shaped like wheat.
He crawled from one to another in the dark
last night and filled his hunger with

the grains. This morning his cries
fall into a rapid squeaking and I lie
on my back in the bed with my hands
looking for each other across my chest.

You lie next to me in the bed hunched
into a curve that avoids touching me.
We have avoided each other in the night
a hot poison spreading on our own centers,

our own screams pounding against our teeth.
Since midnight my mind has scrambled
between walls looking for a drop of water
to put out my dark thirst. Since the

false dawn I have heard the loud sounds
of my pain turn to a steady whimper
behind my eyes and I have heard the animal
I've killed look for a hole in his roof.

Now the sun thuds through the window and
onto the floor and the walls of my throat
close against each other. The first flies
rattle between the wall and ceiling beside

my side of the bed and fart dirty air against
my face as they zip out into the room. I
roll from the bed to the warm tiles and stumble
into the hall and down the wood stairs to

the house below. In the kitchen I find one
glass clean in the litter of last night's
drinking. Two squirrels play in the yard
outside as I try to drink the faucet dry.

THE ARGUMENT

The color of sand and children laughing
rolls into the small radio and the waves
beating themselves in the air above
this hottest afternoon of the summer.

All of this and your stiff back
as I pour the oil on and rub it in
anounces the same theme. We are at war.

Perhaps it was a message I addressed
to the wrong party in a dream at night
or a small piece of machine falling
while I slept late this morning

that forces silence into this space
where only the sun would otherwise be.

But I return it. Sullen for sullen.
Each on his own side of the orange blanket
reading the other's thoughts all wrong,

dry but drowning on a brown summer beach.

The bum in Salt Lake
City shared his last
half buck
with me then I
bought him coffee with
my half he
took me to a movie with
his I
bought him chow mein
afterwards
he bought a
fifth
I paid for
scrambled eggs and
bromo we spent
the last two
cents in a
taxi
riding round and round
the
Great Salt Lake I
would have got
him a pony
but there was
no more
left.

MARCY DARCY STILL GOES TO COLLEGE

I approach the room with the secrecy of an orange tree
and knock at its door. You answer it with the usual
smile on your face. What in hell is the matter with you?

There have been so many fires and your name is unchanged.
Windstorms rip my back from my ribs and you go on smiling.
Coffins wait on the backs of mares and you file your nails.
Kiss. You say Kiss Kiss Kiss and simper through peach pits.

You are an aunt serving tea and I scream Fuck. The tea
tastes the same and you go on about a wedding of zombies
in the back of the house where the dead niggers are kept.

He looked so natural, you say and mold fills the pores
between your teeth. As each window breaks you are reminded

of petals growing on a rose in your ancient backyard.

You have named each one for a national disaster
or a month when you were operated on for the removal of
your ovaries. Look, let me call you Floss or Fanny,

slap you on the ass a lot and open cans of beer. We
can ride off together on an elephant, pretending nothing
has happened. If only you can learn to come the world will

let you live in ignorance and bliss. Just push the right
button. I want to ride you like a sway-backed colt.

My thoughts aren't even here now, just the pauses at the
ends of lines where the typewriter stops. I lie on my back
ripping at my stomach and you want me to stop and

watch your arabesques. When I finally drop you to the bottom of the well you'll probably want to know why.

That isn't the end though, because here we both still are.

TOO

Brown coffee in the morning.
This and that and we talk.
I love your ham and egg smile.
We smoke new postmarks
and that I lie too much.

In my dream I bought a pistol.
You were a bowl of oranges
And I shot b-bs at you
and we both liked that.

The hill is a long way going up.
I smoke too many cigarettes
between here and the new car
but it's fast and low and red.
I need all the help I can get.

If I had a long belted coat
and a low-brim brown hat,
I'd herd goats on hills in Iran
and shoot you in the mouth
as you carried me cups of milk.

The new girl at the office
is long and gray and skinny.
She smells like stale gum.
I don't want her to write my name.
I want a fat iced pear.

THE SEDUCTION

The room is small and loud
and I avoid you
by standing at the piano
looking for fish in my glass.

I watch the wet lights
in the street out the window
while you laugh with your strangers
and touch your soft hair.

It is your long hair
I could reach for and touch.
It would be something for me.
Anyway we will not speak.

The loud night grows fat
and I stand with flat shapes
in corners laughing about
stories they tell about you.

My jaw and my voice are heavy.
I will go home by
myself tired of me.
I will not sleep for hours.

This becomes my way
of talking to you.
This is me looking at you.
It is my brown suit
worn on a cold day.

A LOOSE ROOM

It's kind of a
loose room

I live in

with windows
I can watch birds from

or close
and a door I

walk out
of

or into
depending on
where I stand.

It's kind of a loose room
you've come to,

breaking in
through the left wall

I keep my back to

while
I sleep.

SOME THREE-LINE STANZAS

He is not dead he is sleeping
he has got a job with god.
I have two friends who are not here and I miss them

(in California people write notes to me, they want soft
words, I tell them it is too cold here winter has come in
my teeth)

Today is January.
It's snowed since November.
A long winter is predicted.

This is a line that says help me.
This asks you why not
and this one says thanks

(you may notice
that each of these stanzas
is three lines long)

My mother and father are very old now.
My sister has gray in her hair.
My daughters all talk.

The dogs kill mice by
breaking their backs
with their jaws.

The cats
use
their claws.

He is not dead,
he is sleeping with god
and we are all here together.

It is an open day.
As I walk to the fire I can see
the Marrowback to the east and
the deep hole of the valley
in the west.

Across the road, bricks, scored
by a ruining flame long gone out
and in front of me a barn going to waste.
Last fall it held pheasant
raised like chickens for profit
by the man who also owned
this land I live on
but who gave it up.

At night in the bars in town
men drown each other
in smokey, wet glasses
and the mad eyed girls wonder
who they will go home with

but this is morning and open
and I walk across the yard with
a two-year-old girl in pink pajamas

and hear the wild pheasant cry
his brass sound to the ghosts
of his brothers in the barn
and watch the pregnant husky
chew on the stillborn foal
she brought home last night
her forepaws dyed red with its blood

and you have been waiting now at a table
over this page for all these things
to come together. They will not.

INSTRUCTIONS FOR VIEWING A SOLAR ECLIPSE

"With your back to the sun, hold the paper four or five feet from the
cardboard. The solar image projected onto the paper will be small and
quite faint. . . ."   (UPI feature)

It is against this
thing of sky I lay
my thought momen-
tarily. It is the
darkness and how to
look at it, this a-
voiding of brilliances.

We are in our livingrooms
looking at infinity
on a blue screen. I
sleep off a hangover
upstairs on the couch
and half listen to

the day go out of it-
self in a false cloud.

There is a time when
like today we do not
look at ourselves either,
I have an idea if we did
we would not go blind.

WINTER WALKING FIELDS

November.
The mole goes
to sleep
with the universe.

I walk over
frosted ground
in my new wool shirt.
Rabbits turn
in their warm caves,

hawks tumble
under clouds and
break backs
with their sharp fists
and trees die.

The month is the brown
of old men
tired, cold but
promising sleep.

In the center
of a cleared field
the bones of
a steer
wait for the snow.